for the

love

of a word

Compiled by

Annie Louise
Twitchell

for the dreamers:

your story needs to be told.

tell it.

CONTENTS

ACKNOWLEDGMENTS

Firstly, all these authors need a huge shout-out for their parts. This book would not exist if they hadn't believed in my weird little dream. You are the heart and soul of this book.

Secondly, the Weavers of Words—you know who you are. Without my girls having my back, I wouldn't be where I am. A special thanks to Tammy—you've taken so many of us under your wing, and you're always there when we need you. I hope this book will encourage you.

To the storytellers in my life: thank you.

for the love of a word

Poetry

for the love of a word

4

Eye of the Beholder

In the swirling shadows behind my eyelids,
I see all the most beautiful things in the world.
I see stars in a velvet sky
and butterflies in the dandelions
and birch trees along the riverbank.
When I close my eyes, I see
two cups of coffee on the table
and two jackets on the rack in the hall
and best of all, I see you.

Annie Louise Twitchell

Inkblood

The inkblood flows and scorches through my veins;
it lies barely concealed beneath my skin,
but though invisible, still it remains.

The written word and I may well be kin,
for though I'm made of flesh and he of thought,
we both subsist by inkblood's surge within.

The tie that binds us surely can't be bought;
'tis forged through passion, time, through sweat and tears;
and inkblood tethers all in cords drawn taut.

Though inkblood may flow cold o'er many years,
it lies in wait, 'til inspiration's spark
leaps up again, ignites and once more sears.

When inkblood's cold, then so am I, and dark
are nights when words have fled me just the same.
in dormancy we drift and wait to hark

To inkblood's call to action, to the game
of joining once again to then create
more tales which, through our darkness, truth proclaim.

And when its appetite at last we sate,
the inkblood calms and slows its pulsing flow,
and lets me rest at last, and so I wait

For it to catch me in its undertow
once more, for without it and written word

for the love of a word

for company, no solace do I know.

Tempestuous our quest is, and absurd,
but I would not abandon it for aught,
lest e'en one shred of truth be left unheard.

The inkblood surges deep within, and ought,
for how else to express what's in my mind?
What might be lost, if inkblood scorched me not?

So I will heed its call, and let it bind
me to the written word whene'er it calls,
lest lost ones, by my silence, be left blind.

My inkblood flows not for me, but for all
who by my word and witness might be reached;
extends from Adonai's most fervent call,

For how shall any learn, unless I teach?
And how shall they believe unless they hear
what inkblood, word, and I form into speech?

So ask why I endure the inkblood's sear.
I'll say, "Because my Author put it there."

C.F. Barrows

Words Unsaid

I miss you.
I try to tell myself that I don't, but I do.
You haunt my dreams.
You plague my thoughts.
When I hear your name, my heart beats faster.
When you're near, it flutters and aches.
And when I see you moving on without me, it dies in my chest.

I wish I knew how to forget you, but you have changed me so utterly that I fear I would not recognize myself.
I wish I could matter to you, or learn some way to stop letting you matter to me.
I miss you with every fiber of my being, every war-torn scrap of my soul.
But with almost as much conviction, I believe that it is hopeless.

You do not miss me.
When you sleep, my face never makes an appearance in your dreams.
When you close your eyes again to picture your future, I have no part in it.
We no longer share a path, you and I.

Oh, but how my heart longs to purge the truth.
To run to you, though I know you do not wait for me.
To spill out my heart, though I know you would keep yours locked inside your chest.
To wait for you, though I know that one day, perhaps very

for the love of a word

soon, you will take that guarded heart out of your chest and give it to someone else.

We have no future, you and I... but oh, how I wish we did.

C. F. Barrows

Soul-Thoughts

Words are the soul of the Wordsmith.
One cannot be separated from the other
without ripping both apart,
dividing sinew from bone
and body from soul.

Words are the breath of the Wordsmith.
To suppress and conceal them
is to smother air in the lungs,
to step into the vacuum of space
and swallow nothingness.

Words are the heart of the Wordsmith,
a living, beating organ of dreams.
To hold them back
is to hoard embers in a box
until they explode.

Words are the life of the Wordsmith.
To release them is to *be,*
so hold nothing back,
a flood of soul-thoughts
for thirsty bookworms.

Savannah Jezowski

I Need Your Story

I need your story
the way a child needs a mother,
the way a ship needs a sea to rest on
and a breeze to fill her sails.

I need your words
the way breath needs a body to fill,
the way a clock needs time to tell it
which way to turn its hands.

I need your soul
the way morning needs a sunrise,
the way waves need the tide to turn them
toward the waiting shore.

I need your story
the way my heart needs fresh blood
to keep it beating, pumping, living
'til the last page is turned.

Savannah Jezowski

Sky Paper

Beneath a harvest moon,
blood red and rising,
when no one else will listen
and you stand alone with shadows,
searching the darkness
for a kindred ear, a soul mate—
peel back the purple night and see
that the nymphs in the grasses
and sprites in the hollows
are standing up on tiptoe,
listening.

Leave your manufactured cage
and follow the serpent's trail
that warps through the forest
to where the fire faerie dance
around a florescent fire,
spinning tales
about the Goblin King
and his ghost-gray mountain.
Take out your ember pen,
let it set fire to the page
and burn into your soul
forever.

Write it out on the sky,
where the lava sun
sets in the heavens.
Let it thunder in your ears
like beating drums in the desert
and echo in your heart

for the love of a word

where no one ever visits.
Pour it out on paper,
let it bleed into the ink,
and burn into your soul
forever.

Savannah Jezowski

MUSE

I know I haven't been around much.
I'm in that place—you know the one,
that place
where all is murky and uninspired—
too tired to think, too sad to dream.
The words won't come.
Sleep is empty, dreamless,
exhausted.

I see you sitting, pen idle, waiting.
If I could, I'd come and fill you with dreams.
I love your words,
how you take me and form me
into beautiful thoughts.
But just now, I can't be formed—
too scarred, too brittle,
too invisible.

I know I haven't been around much,
but don't give up on me.
I'll come back.
I always come back
because you are mine, and I am yours.
I love the way you make me more than I am,
more than scars, more than brittle,
more than nothing.

Without your pen, I'd be just a scent on the wind,
a stagnant pond with no outlet,
an invisible face in a mirror—

for the love of a word

less than a memory
because I never was.
So wait for me:
I want to fill a book
and live.

Savannah Jezowski

Deaf Ears

Silence,
thick and tangible,
a murky, smothering void.
No one seems to hear your words,
but keep writing because, somewhere,
someone needs the words you're trying to share.
They are searching in the pain-riddled void,
surrounded by thousands who don't hear
their silent plea for help, for comfort.
So keep on writing, and sharing,
because someone hears you,
and you share your pain
through words.

Savannah Jezowski

Don't Give Up

If God gave up because people failed Him,
the world would have ended after Adam.

If Beethoven gave up when he lost his hearing,
"The Ninth Symphony" wouldn't exist.

If Beatrix Potter gave up when rejected,
Peter Rabbit wouldn't be a children's classic.

If Madeleine L'Engle gave up after 25 rejections,
A Wrinkle in Time would never have been published.

If you give up because of the obstacle before *you*,
your masterpiece may never be written.

So never give up:
your best is yet to come.

Savannah Jezowski

An Author's Prayer

God has a purpose
a perfect, holy way:
He lays a plot before me
and asks me to obey.
Sometimes the themes are steeper
than I ever thought they'd be.
Lord, help me to follow
even when I cannot see!

Help me to follow,
when I begin to stumble;
Help me to trust You,
when the words begin to crumble.
Help me to listen
and to quietly be still,
to heed Your every whisper,
to seek Your holy will.

God has a purpose
a perfect, holy way.
He lays a story before us
and asks us to obey.
Even when the books are steeper
than we ever thought they'd be,
Lord, help us to follow
even when we cannot see.

Savannah Jezowski

Perseverance

her depression

made her sleep

while her school work

sat undone

her anxiety

gave her nightmares

and fears of dying

it was all so much

she hardly felt like trying

but her God

prodded her on

kept her going

she put pen to paper

she wrote a book

while her anxiety and depression

simply looked

Annie Harley

The Stories Know

I can see the creases of untold stories, strained across your eyes.
The way you hide them behind your eyeglasses, just out of view,
Tells me how insecure, they lead you to feel.

The stories are screaming, scowling, and begging to break free.
They've been resilient and rebellious from the moment they hatched.
They never submit to the authority you set, still they long for control.

You, the creator, still awake in the wee hours of night,
bending and shoving your creativity into that which the world would enjoy.
Insanity edges near—you can't quite bring your ideas to life.

See,
it's always been
far simpler than that.

Unclench those fists.
Relax your eyes.
Surrender.

The stories know what to do.
They will tell themselves.
Allow them to lead you.

Rachel Katherine

The Senses of Writing

The crinkling sound of paper, and *'thunk'*, as yet another is tossed away—the sound of failure.

You and I know it well.

Delicate fingers, stained with ink and tears—the sign of struggle.

You and I know them well.

The jagged edges of a worn out desk, strewn with all sorts of clutter—the feeling of creative labor.

You and I know it well.

Oh, the aroma of a story, freshly baked.
Not overdone, nor undercooked;
expression and artistry brought to new levels of talent.

You and I may not know it well.

Pinky swears, and half-hearted promises, agree on one thing:
One day, you will know it well.

For now, you mix ingredients,
and experiment with flavors.

Rachel Katherine

Squandered

Painted proses and reckless roses.

Did I not tell her that one day, it'll settle?

Stories shifting on their own and novels nodding off to sleep.

What if she gave up, too?

Olive-flavored outlines with cocktails made of coffee.

Has she disappeared?

Haiku lined with hatchets and letters penned in lavender.

Oh my, it seems she's fled her occupation.

Desk dying and chair crying.

Does she know what she's left behind?

Rachel Katherine

ESCAPING
REALITY.

Selina J. Eckert

for the love of a word

24

Letters

for the love of a word

for **the love of** a word

for the love of a word

for the love of a word

Writer

noun

writ·er | \ ˈrī-tər \

A caffeine dependent organism

1. Someone in search of completion, healing, or otherwise wholeness.

2. An irregular-shaped figure, with great potential for destruction or creation (approach with caution)

3. A creature with the mind of a jellyfish, and the hands of a koala bear.

Rachel Katherine

Some Words of Advice

Writers and children have many things in common. For example, both have the attention span of a sleep deprived squirrel. Parents and friends try their best to regulate the caffeine and sugar intake of such species, but all attempts are futile. Writers and children respond strongly to such food items.

As a child stacks jenga blocks, only to tear them down in the same breath, so a writer builds its manuscripts, sky high, only to hide them beneath the floorboards.

Studies show, that both writers and children are better left to their odd ways. Both creatures are easily upset and disturbed.

If, for any reason, you must approach one, I highly recommend you bring tribute of some kind.Preferably a gift, such as a small toy or pen, but anything will do.

Best of luck to you, it's no easy task.

If, for whatever reason you are unsuccessful, you may call the authorities using the toll-free number listed on the back of your neck.

Thanks, and have a great day!

Rachel Katherine

for the love of a word

Dear writer, comrade, friend,

Your words matter.

Your story matters.

You never know who will read your story, and how much it will mean to them. Maybe a side character will remind your reader of their sister. Maybe they will experience the same emotion as the main character in that one scene and feel less alone. Maybe it will help your reader be more understanding. Maybe they will need an escape for a day, stuck on a train. The human experience is vast, and there will always be too few books, too few voices sharing words.

You have a unique angle to the world. We all do. Help us understand what it means to be you.

I have always wondered what it would be like to be someone else for a day. Have different problems, different strengths. Books can help with that.

I have also felt so very alone. You probably have at some point, too. Write your story so that everyone can feel just a little bit less alone.

Write.

It makes a difference.

Rebecca Woodie

for the love of a word

My Dear Author,

YOU ARE AWESOME!!!

Not only did you spend all those hours sifting through research, all those hours of making sure your locations made sense geographically, all those hours making sure you didn't give too much detail about the landscape so you wouldn't bore them but trying to convey exactly what your mind pictured the scenery as being...

Not only did you go through endless baby name sites searching for the elusive perfect name for your favorite character, and spend countless days coming up with backstories and personalities for each character that would define who they are to a T, and spend many a sleepless night trying to figure out exactly how person A would react to person B stealing their box of muffins when they knew perfectly well that those banana chocolate chip muffins were NOT FOR YOU, CHAD, NOT FOR YOU—ahem, sorry about that. Anyway, as I was saying...

Not only did you have many conversations with fellow writers, family, and friends to make sure what you first thought was a good idea actually was (which it was, you just needed reassurance), and not only did you admit sometimes your idea for the book wasn't as great as you thought and took a pair of scissors to your precious book, and not only did you connect every dot and check most scrupulously for loopholes...

Not only did you cry, sweat, giggle, groan, sigh, and shake your head as your characters, at times, took it upon themselves to write your story the way they pleased (do they ever really follow orders?)...

Not only did you go through the terrifying process of editing, proof reading, designing covers, all that legal stuff, and then finally press that last button or sign that last paper that officially made you a published author...

You did it well.

You made it through. You worked hard, and now have the reward. You wrote your own book, how you wanted it to be written, and can now proudly look at a book that bears your name on the cover.

I'm proud of you! You survived the crazy process that is called writing a book! Your novel is going to be read by who knows how many people. It will be loved by some, adored by others. Oh, true, a critic or two, maybe some negative reviews might come along, but if they don't like it, it doesn't matter. You have people who do.

You are someone's favorite author. Your book is someone's favorite book that they hug tight to their chest after reading. Those hours, days, months, and years of work have paid off in the form of a book that will inspire future writers.

You did just fine. Give yourself a pat on the back, go get some tea, take a break for just a moment...

Then go do it again. I know you can, you've

already done it once before. Now there's nothing to stop you from doing a great job once more.

A Fellow Writer,

Melissa Holliday

for the love of a word

My Dearest *New to The World of Writing* Author,

Let me start off by saying... don't rush yourself, okay? Yes, it's good to set deadlines, but you're only going to stress yourself out if you set a million of them. Don't stress yourself out. Just enjoy your writing. It'll all come together when you least expect it to.

Do yourself a favor, and don't delete anything. You'll be glad you didn't banish those early manuscripts to those childish stories you first started writing. One day, you might look at them and laugh, or you might see a diamond hidden in the dirt and decide it's time to work on them again. I can't begin to tell you how cool your readers are going to think it is when you give them little snippets from these beginning books you wrote.

Yes, it feels like what you're writing will never reach any shelves, but you and I both know that's not true. Yes, that name is a great choice for your main character. Yes, you *can* name your fictional world anything you want because it's your book. Yes, you should take into account that forty-seven named characters with backstories as individual as snowflakes will require you and your readers to pay attention, but it's your book, dear, and you can write it however you want. Yes, you can do this.

By the way, those critics? Yes, they're going to be there for the whole of your writing career. And you know what? That's okay. You can't have a biggest fan if you don't have a few critics along the way. Just because someone doesn't like what you wrote does not mean it is garbage or that you're not a talented writer, okay? It simply means your book wasn't right for them, just like you've read books that weren't your taste. It's okay to feel down when you get a negative review, to cry even, but don't let it discourage you or keep you down, friend. You're writing books because you want to, how you want to, for people who want to read them. If someone doesn't like what you wrote, they don't have to read it. It's as simple as that.

And, yes, you will have fans. They'll be small in number at the start, but they're going to grow. Fan clubs are going to be started for your books. Imagine that! Someone is going to sketch out what they imagine your characters to look like. People are going to beg you to make your books into a movie—not that you always should, since we all know the book is always better than the movie. But indulge these sweet fans with hope that one day YOUR BOOK WILL BE IN A THEATER! Fans are going to want to meet you and get your autograph and have you sign their books. You're going to be followed on social media and have fledgling writers coming to you for advice.

That's exciting, right? Know what else is exciting? The fact that your mind is full of hundreds, if not thousands or millions, of potential stories and characters. You'll live a thousand different lives through your characters. Experience places you might never see with your own eyes. Learn a hundred careers and earn degrees in studies you never stepped foot in a classroom to learn. You're going to solve crimes, match starry-eyed lovers, create entire worlds, slay dragons, defeat enemies, and find happily ever afters. All of that? It all is coming from your mind, from your heart... from you.

for the love of a word

You're awesome. You've got talent. Now, go write. Don't just sit there daydreaming about fans or stressing over imaginary critics. Go be someone's future favorite, awesome author!

A Fellow Writer,

Melissa Holliday

for the love of a word

Dear Writer,

You are the only one who can write your story. You count. Your ideas matter. Your voice is needed.

Always start writing. Just start wherever you need to. Just write.

You don't need a final draft the first time. The first time, just write it all down. That's the job of the first draft: to be written.

It is so much easier to sort through everything later, to see what fits the narrative you wish to convey. The revising, the rearranging, the editing –you can have as much help as you wish with those parts. Only you, though, can tell your story. Just start writing.

There's light to be found in the darkness. Tell the story, even if it hurts. It's so much better to let the pain flow out than to keep it locked within.

Find a good pen or a good font, and start writing.

Kathy Twitchell

Don't Wait for a Maybe-One-Day

When I was younger, before I met my husband, before I had been perpetually single, I started a hope chest with my mom. I went to the store with my family, who bought my sister and me each an identical, large, teal and purple chest... and a stack of tumblers in our favorite colors— the first deposit to be made.

I don't know how many families do this, did this, or will continue this tradition in the future, but this hope chest was our way of dreaming of what may come, what we hoped our lives would one day be. It was something both my mother and grandmother had done when they were young, and they were beyond excited to help us start ours.

Besides the cups, my mom bought us other kitchen goods (which we never actually used when we finally got our first apartment) and had us pack away some of our favorite toys after we outgrew them, just in case we needed them for future children. My grandmother told us of the pink and black linens she had embroidered for her own hope chest years ago, a color scheme she had wanted in her first home, then gave us kitschy holiday decorations for our future homes. Every year another relative would give us something else to put in our hope chests.

For years, I made hope deposits into this chest— things I wanted for my future life, my married life, my "maybe one day" children. For years, the women in my family gave me more items to add to the chest.

And for years they gathered dust.

In my writing life, it was much the same. I grew up with such a love of the written word that not only did I spend my free time reading and dreaming myself into the stories, but I attempted to write my own.

When I was young, I would draw elaborate covers, write a Chapter One, and then let the scrap paper become lost in time. As I got older and learned how to use a word processor, I spent my days and years creating beautiful documents for manuscripts I never finished, dreaming about the day I might one day be a published author, and waiting for inspiration to strike me.

For all those years, I didn't complete a single manuscript.

Then, one year early in my adult life, I read a book with some friends. And I will never forget, or fail to use, this one piece of advice that changed my outlook completely: Don't save the good china. Don't save and store away things you love for a rainy day or a maybe eventually. That day may never come. So use them now. Enjoy them now. Work for what you want *now*.

This idea has continued to spread and grow in my life the past few years. Why keep around hopes and dreams (and actual good china) for a rainy day or for when there's more time? Why not just buy the things or use the good china or work on the dreams you actually want instead of wasting time dreaming and waiting?

During graduate school (in an unrelated field), it took three extra years of stress for me to realize how much I loved to write, how much I wanted to be a writer, and that I had to start taking it seriously if I was ever going to do anything with this dream. Why should I wait to complete my degree before advancing my dreams of being a writer?

For the first time in my life, the deposits stopped as— incredibly— I questioned why I was waiting and saving up for an uncertain future. Why was I putting off my life until life settled down or gave me more time or threw me inspiration? Until I felt like I was ready?

I was dreaming about the future I wanted and telling myself, and everyone else, what I wanted to do, what I wanted to be. But I wasn't doing anything about it. I told myself I'd try when school was over, when my schedule was lighter, or when I had more experience. But school went on for an extra four years after I graduated with my Bachelor's, my schedule just kept getting busier, and I never even began teaching myself what I thought I needed to know in order to start.

Why was that? Why was I waiting to do what I loved when I could start *now*? Why was I stopping myself from enjoying everything life had to offer me *right now*? Why was I putting off those first steps to living the life I wanted for myself? Just because I felt like I wasn't ready or it would take time and work?

If everyone waited until they felt ready, allowed themselves to be lulled into inaction by the fear of the time and work, the whole world would be stuck in a state of stasis, never doing anything significant or trying anything difficult. All they would do is hope and dream.

Hopes and dreams are great, but they can only get you so far. It took me so long to figure that out that by the time I started taking my dream of becoming an author seriously, I had lost my chance for several manuscripts I will never finish.

So I started doing the work. I learned, and I wrote, and I dreamed about fictional worlds in every spare moment. I was finally coming to understand that if I packed my things, and my dreams, away in the hope of a future I wanted, they would all crumble to dust before it happened. I had to take the steps to create that future, to make the life I hoped for instead of merely wishing and dreaming.

Don't get me wrong, dear writer. You still must dream, and dream big. Imagine what it would be like to spend your days creating. Picture your books on the big screen. Think of yourself at that book signing.

But while you are dreaming, don't forget to take steps forward. If you don't create your own future, make your dreams start working for the space they take up in your head, nothing will ever happen. No one is going to just hand it to you.

for the love of a word

So start now. Learn, and carve out your own time. Don't wait for inspiration; it's too fickle to be reliable. Make the life you want, make the worlds you want. Be an active participant in your dreams, and make the deposits count for something.

Don't save your dreams away for a maybe-one-day.

Selina J. Eckert

Your Secret

You've hidden it well, but it has grown beyond your reach. No longer do you carry it inside your chest, confining its energy to the meter of your heartbeat. It has long since enclosed you, a stanza under lock and key, a room layered brick by brick, line by line. I see it. I see it in the way metaphors fall like rain from your fingers yet dam up in your mouth when you speak. I see it when pages flick by beneath your gaze—a gaze hungry for tales, for memories. I see it in the way your breath caesuras at hidden pearls of prose, your exhale an echo of the stories you want to create.

But I know more than even this. I have heard every torn page, every crumpled letter, every furious erasure you make, hoping to scrub your lines clean of your work. A stain of hopeless mediocrity, you call it. I've heard how you sigh. I taste the bitter tonguefuls, briny with impatience, as you start again, again, again—never satisfied with your work. Never satisfied with yourself.

After hours and hours, your hands turn to leathery dolphin skin, coated with the grey sheen of graphite. Your page is an empty white sea.

Your secret is a two-pronged trident, its wound piercing fathoms deep: *you are a writer, but you don't believe it.*

When you are asked about your writing, there is something adrift behind your eyes. I know that look. I know the thinness in your voice when you answer: *yes, yes, I'm a writer.*

for the love of a word

You think yourself a liar. Your mind whispers cold doubts to you, tells you that being a true writer is something noble, something enigmatic. How could it be this scratched-out rhythm of papers cuts and half-forgotten ideas? A true writer, you think, carves beautiful monuments from words, bends rhythms and upswellings of unseen voices to her will with the tip of her pen. A true writer rides the fiercest of storms, while you stand scared in this ankle-deep pool of tepid inspiration. When you are asked about it, your smile disintegrates, fragile as sea foam. You hide your notebook in your pocket, and tell yourself that if no one can see it, you will not have to talk about it.

Sometimes the notebook remains tucked out of sight for so long, your forget about it. Not forever, no. But long enough that when a book falls open to a page vibrant with words, that old wound aches anew. Because oh, oh, you remember—you remember this feeling.

You begin again; you always do. Then once more, and once more after that, like the endless return of the tide to the shore.

Someday, you will learn to trust yourself with this secret.

You will learn that the story you carry is weightless only after you tether its sails to paper, when you let it berth in the spiral-bound realms hidden within your desk. You will learn to trust that the allusions and enjambments are more than just tangled nets in your head, and after years of weaving them into your verse, the waves of words will settle into place.

for the love of a word

Someday, every scratch and swirl of your pen will settle into its place, its home. I can already hear its rhythm—the rising and falling, the wild tidal wave dance of words and images, receding at whispers of doubt, rising and falling, day in and day out.

And when you find yourself drenched by the tsunami of your own ballads—remember. Remember the moments your voice was gone, when the stories ran dry, when you couldn't taste the salty spray of inspiration. These are a part of your rhythm, the crests and currents of your being. These are part of your secret.

Abigail M. Swanson

for the love of a word

To The Extroverted Writer:

You don't remember a time when you didn't write stories. From the youngest age memory can recall, you were writing and illustrating stories for all of your friends so they could enjoy them. You wrote because you had to, and you wrote because you loved to see others smile.

But when others stopped smiling, you stopped writing for a time.

No, you never stopped writing, but secretly hid what you wrote. Because, how could you stop the influx of words that always flooded your brain and heart?

Those childhood stories became poems depicting the dark natures of betrayal and hate you received. You couldn't share your poems. Darkness without light can never make one smile. You needed your joy again, but even more you needed someone to trust.

Carefully, you opened yourself up to a world of new people and with those new people come new words and new ideas. You wrote new stories for them. You shared your words and your heart with those people.

And they hated you and your words.

"You are a talented writer wasting your words on nonsense."

Their words crushed *your* words for a time.

But you aren't easily defeated. Once more you rise and you write and you share.

You believe in the stories that God lays on your heart. You will keep writing. God tells you that there is someone out there. Someone who will smile, with tears in their eyes.

And so with that promise, you continue to write.

You find other writers. Some of them are like you, but most of them are not. They say things like, "You don't have to write to be a writer."

But you knew that isn't true. If you ever stop writing, your words will die—and so will you.

They say, "You might be a writer if you binge watch Netflix late into the early morning."

Or, "You might be a writer if you own piles of chocolate."

Or, "You might be a writer if you prefer books to people."

But you know that makes as much sense as saying, "The sky is pink because trees are purple."

No, a writer is a dreamer that never sleeps, though yearning for rest. Anyone can watch Netflix, eat chocolate, or hide from society. But only a writer will always be burdened with words that need to see the light of a smile.

Your smile. *Their* smiles.

One day those smiles come. It is a beautiful day indeed, and on that day you know that you'll never stop writing, despite all the hate that might and *will* still claw at your soul.

You become the writer who is serious about actually writing. You pull out of your shell of worries and release your heart every day. Sometimes only a few words will come. But the more you write each day, the more those words grow in number.

Your one story becomes another story and another and another and another, until there are more than all your unfinished stories combined.

This encourages you.

But what encourages you the most are the smiles. Because while others write for themselves, you write for God's people.

You write to edify, to encourage, to entertain. And in trade, God allows your own heart to be edified, encouraged, and entertained. You learn and so do they. You cry and so do they. You laugh and so do they.

There are still haters, but they are drowned out by your success . . . and doubts.

You love writing, yes. God made you to write, yes. And there are those that are touched by your words.

But . . . can you truly be serious about doing this forever? Can you write enough to make your words worth your time? Are your words really good enough for all the time you give them? And what if you never publish anything?

You wonder if maybe you might be wasting your time.

Because a serious person has goals no matter what they do. And to be published seems too far into a future of impossibilities.

Maybe you should pursue something more *stable*.

And for those short dark moments of despair it seems much easier to just give into to the hype of watching Netflix, eating chocolate, and hiding.

Instead, you push yourself further out there.

You choose discomfort over darkness. You choose long hours of staring at a screen,typing and learning, over movies and media. You choose a long walk for fresh air and inspiration rather than a bar of chocolate.

And you meet people. And they meet your words.

And they smile.

And you are given the energy to keep on writing.

You choose to seriously pursue your dream past the point of exhaustion. Food? Sleep? Fun? They do not matter, only your stories.

But through this all you nearly forget something *very* important. You forget why you started writing.

You aren't writing to become successful. *(But, you argue, isn't it? If my words don't "make it" how can I logically keep on writing?)*

for the love of a word

You aren't writing for yourself. *(Remember the years of your dark poetry. You never want to return to such despair.)*

You have always written for others, to help them embrace, *not escape* the reality God has placed humanity. Money doesn't matter when you have a calling. The future is of no importance when God says live *now*.

You have nearly forgotten to live the story God has placed you in, forgetting your own reality and your friends around you.

But you remember, and for a time you leave the story you are writing to laugh with your friends and to live your *own* story. Your life wasn't meant to be ruled by your words, but by God's words.

And so you write . . . but you live, too. Unless you love and laugh with God and man, how else will you know the words to make your stories breathe?

You have learned much, Dear Extroverted Writer, but you still have much to learn.

But I believe that as long as you hold onto these treasured lessons you can face all that the future yells at you. You will keep writing and sharing. And your stories will make the world smile.

You now know that hate will not kill you; but the hurt you rise from will be coals to flame your story.

You will love and your story will shine.

Because you are a writer that is brave enough to

for the love of a word

never drop the pen.

Keturah Lamb

for the love of a word

My dear fellow writers,

Do you know what you are?

No, this is not some deep philosophical question meant to make you question your existence in this life. This is a question to make you think about what it is that you do.

You are a writer. You are a person that puts words onto a page.

Yet you are doing so much more than that.

Each carefully chosen word on your page is contributing to something bigger. You are creating something. Creating worlds, people, personalities, ideas, and stories.

With some words you can create a picture of how a character looks within the reader's mind. With other words you can tell the reader of the character's personality. The story you tell shows the reader who the character is. The very character of the character.

As you do that you are also creating emotion, not only for the character, but also for the reader. The reader laughs and feels happiness. The reader cries and becomes angry. It is no longer about facts, but emotions. Stories don't just stimulate the brain, but pull at the heart.

As soon as you have accomplished that, you have opened up a whole new world of opportunity. Having a connection to your reader's heart means they now connect to your ideas. The reader understands something new, something that can affect how they think and how they act.

In short, you can have an impact on your readers with the power of words.

Please don't abuse this power. Use it as an opportunity to change the world. To have an impact for the good of others.

But please don't be intimidated by this power either. Intimidation leads to a very slow rate of producing each amazing word, or an inability to start at all. At that point, the purpose and reason for writing is gone.

However, do not take this wonderful ability lightly. Each word that you use to influence someone towards something wrong or evil does come back on you. You aren't responsible for another person's actions, but you are responsible for the influence you have over them.

With each word that can create something beautiful, there are words that can create something terrible. Choose these words wisely. Choose them with care.

Because the more words you write, the more power you gain. Power that your vilest character envies and that your most timid character fears.

So go, and release that power to the world. Use each word to bring joy and sadness. Use it to bring awareness. Use it to create role models and standards.

for the love of a word

Use the power of your words to change the world.

Lauren Grinder

Remains

I remember when I found you. You were all
bleeding fingers and fairytales, carrying the constellations
in your eyes. You bent over the page and excess words
whispered weaves of smoke, tendrilling into the air around
you. You fed my fragmenting soul on tales of mermaids,
chipmunks, and girls who made friends with spiders.

I watched you grow as I faded. My limbs crackled
in the firelight, my spine breaking with the failing logs, and
I taught you all the things I knew, all the things you
couldn't understand.

I taught you—the words are not what make the
story. I held your small hands in my own, guided them
through each letter, whispered the shapes into your ear. I
told you each letter made a word, each word made a
sentence, but it was not words that made a story. Not
words but you. You bled out your soul before I could
create a single sentence, and the blood on the page was
your own, not mine. Mine dried up long ago.

I taught you—the worlds must crawl out of your
pages. I kneaded your fingers against the images clutched
between your temples until you were strong enough to
loose them on your own. You pushed my hands away and
left trembling newborn governments in your wake. Soft
puffs of breath from your lungs, and the borealis set
aflame.

I taught you—the characters must be as real to
you as your own self. You told me the world wasn't ready
for that. My lips cracked open, raw, swollen when I smiled.

for the love of a word

I hope I told you, you were right.

You told me the news, sent me pages bound in stone, wrapped in light. I held your pages in shaking, shadowy fingers, pressed my nose to the crisp furrows of text to see if I could breathe in your sweat and tears. But there were none to be found in layers of fresh ink.

I'm so proud of you I could die, I whispered. You thanked me, and my heart disintegrated.

What's next? you asked. You weren't even watching, when my skin sunk into my bones, and I stroked your cheek with skeletal appendages. You felt the cold of the ring on my finger, but not the scratch of my bones against your flesh, too engrossed in the words pouring out of your soul.

Whatever you want, my dear, I whispered. My last words, as I pressed non-existent lips against your hair. You didn't even flinch.

Someday, you'll cup my ashes in your fingers, stare at them with those fading constellations. You'll ask me what's next, and this time, I won't answer. You might cry; I don't know. I don't know how long will pass, if you'll have a student of your own, if you'll still bleed out words, if you'll have a single tear left.

But your soul—the carnivorous butterfly flitting in your chest—it will know what to do, even as it devours your mind. When that day comes, you'll breathe life into my remains, create a whole world with nothing but ashes and air. The angels will hold their breath in awe, watch you raise tender worlds to life, and I—from heaven—will smile, hold your newborns in clean, strong hands, and whisper in your ear, *I knew you could do it.*

C.S. Taylor

for the love of a word

Dear Writer,

Are you spying on me? Your last book was perfect!

It was everything I didn't know I needed; it was real.

I felt. I wept. I laughed. I healed.

Thank you for pouring your heart onto paper, that my heart might find it and be touched.

Sincerely,

A Reader

Katherine Brown

for the love of a word

Dear Writer,

Thank you.

Thank you for writing a book I loved.

Thank you for writing a book I didn't care for.

Thank you for writing that tedious how-to manual.

Thank you for your passion to put pen to page.

Thank you for your perseverance; it encourages hope inside me.

Thank you for bravely publishing your brainchild; it gives me courage to do the same.

Thank you for enduring the criticism & the edits to produce a good piece; it shows me the path.

Thank you for your success; it feeds my dreams.

Sincerely,

A Beginning Writer

Katherine Brown

for the love of a word

Dear Writer,

Writing is hard work. If you've been writing for any length of time, then you understand this truth. Maybe you understand it better than most, or maybe you're just slowly beginning to understand it.

Writing requires diligence, perseverance, and the ability to bleed your heart onto paper. It requires you to paint images of color with simple words of black and white. It requires resilience beyond what we think we can bear. It takes tears and hurt and rejection and all of those yucky things we'd sometimes rather not associate with our dreams.

But you...*you do it all beautifully.*

Even without knowing you, I know this. Because let's be honest, you wouldn't be reading this book if you didn't take your writing seriously. You wouldn't stick with your project past the first week if you weren't really serious that this...*this is what you were meant to do.*

And perhaps that's what I want you to hold onto most of all, dear writer.

You were meant for this.

Through all of the hard, discouraging moments of a writer's journey, it can be so easy to feel as if you somehow took a wrong turn. Should I really be feeling this way—discouraged, frustrated, and a little bit uncertain—if

I was meant to write? If I was meant to write and pursue this dream, then why does it sometimes feel a whole lot more like work than it does dreaming?

All dreams require work. And at some point, all dreams make us feel a little bit exhausted and frustrated. At some point, they always feel a little bit more like work than we first expected them to.

But dreamers don't ever lose their passion because they know…*this dream is bigger than them.*

And as a writer, you are a dreamer. All writers are. They're dreamers with their eyes wide open and their fingers glued to the keyboard. *That's what you are.*

You were made for this and I wish I could look into your eyes as I remind you…God *didn't put this story in your heart just because.* He has a purpose. For you. For your book. For the story in your heart aching to be told on paper. He has a purpose for all of it and that's why He made you for this.

Because only *you* can tell the story He has written in your heart to tell. Only *you* can give to the world what He has written in your story to give.

You were meant for this.

For the long nights where the words and images float through your mind, preventing any sleep. For the hours in front of the computer screen until your mind feels numb. For the finger cramps because you've been typing for too long. For the overwhelming joy that pours out of your heart when you type the final words on the project that took your heart and soul.

Even for the discouragement that shapes you into a stronger writer. For the discipline it takes to keep writing even when you suddenly don't feel like it one day. For the pain that comes with rejection but that fuels you to keep going no matter what.

He made you for all of it.

And you, dear writer, were born to tell a story that only you can tell.

Tell it.

With love from,
Another writer

Isabella Morganthal

Dear Writer,

I can still remember the day I received my first rejection letter.

I can still remember the way my heart dropped to the floor as I pulled my knees up to my chest and allowed the salty tears to drip off the bottom of my chin.

To me, rejection meant I had failed. It meant I was not good enough. It meant my dreams were never going to come true.

And I didn't just get one rejection letter for my writing. *I got several.*

How did that translate to me? I was not good enough to ever be a writer.

If you've been writing for any length of time and faced your first writing rejection, then you've probably believed that lie too. And oh friend, do I know how damaging that lie is.

That's why I'm writing this letter to you today. Because I want to cup your chin in my hands and whisper a truth to you that will change how you view rejection forever…

Rejection is God's redirection to your purpose for His glory. Rejection is not just a delay. It's purposeful.

And here's why I believe you're going to come out of rejection stronger than before: *Because when God calls you to something, He's going to give you the strength to keep on keeping on, even when it's hard.*

Your role is to keep writing. *To keep trying.*

Send in thirty manuscripts or articles or stories and if all thirty get rejected, then you better believe you need to write another thirty and try again. You try until the doors open. You write until you get the acceptance letter. Because I know...*I know it's going to come.* You just have to keep writing for it.

You can't give up here. You can't quit. I know it's easy to just forget it all and set your writing aside. I know it's hard—*so hard*—to keep writing when you feel that heavy weight of rejection lying on your chest. But right around the corner is your breakthrough. Right around the corner is the moment you've been waiting for.

God doesn't waste anything. Not even the hardest rejection you have faced or are still going to face. He wants to use it. Use it to make you stronger, more resilient, more determined.

But you have to be brave enough to keep going.

I know you can. I know you've got it in you. I believe that with all of my heart. That certainly doesn't mean it's going to be easy, and it certainly doesn't mean you won't have those days where you pull your knees up to your chest and watch the salty tears drip off the bottom of your chin.

But it does mean that I know you'll have the courage to push through those moments. That you'll find the courage—*in Him*—to stand to your feet, wipe away the tears, and try again.

Write another story. Send another email. Look for what you have to learn from the next rejection. Bravely fight for your dream.

You can do it. With all of my heart I believe that.

Friend, you were born a writer. *A little rejection isn't going to take that away.*

With love from,
Another writer

Isabella Morganthal

for the love of a word

Dear Writer,

I've always loved being called a writer. There's something about that word, something whimsical and fantastic, something the word *novelist* or *author* simply doesn't possess.

But at the same time as I loved being called a writer, I struggled with it. I felt like I didn't write enough to justify it. I was working on a book, sure, but since I was in middle school and high school, my writing time was sporadic and, generally, far shorter than I wanted it to be. There were stretches where I didn't write *at all*. I was uncomfortable labeling myself as a writer—a word that held so much power for me—because there were days it made me feel like an absolute fraud.

I'm still in high school as I write this. There are still times that I don't get to write as much as I want to—because I'm working, or doing homework, or hanging out with friends, or filling out college applications, or any of the other billion things that take up my time.

Here's the thing, friend. I *love* writing. But I also love a lot of other things. And I only get to be in high school, with a limited amount of responsibility, once.

So I'm cautioning you not to spend all your time writing. A writer is a writer, no matter how often they write. I always have story ideas buzzing around my head— how to fix that plot hole, how to make that relationship feel more real, a new project entirely. And writing is good for me. It's a way to find out what I'm feeling, to have a record of my thoughts.

for the love of a word

Writing is a wonderful thing.

But it isn't everything.

At least, it shouldn't be.

Sometimes writing is crazy and magical and every word you write feels like pure gold. And those times? They're the best. Hang onto them. Because you're going to go through times where writing is work and where you'll have to force yourself to sit down and think of words. And that's okay, too. It's okay to take a break. There are seasons of life where you just can't write, which can feel like the end of the world.

But they're not.

Because when you come back (because as a writer, you'll *always* come back) you'll be astounded at what you are capable of, and you will have more new, fresh ideas.

No season—not even a dry one—lasts forever.

Your passion will return. And you will be stronger for surviving the drought.

Wishing you the best,

Emily Vedder

for the love of a word

Dear Writer,

I remember when I first realized that writing was stressful. Not in a casual, offhand way, where it's stressful when you work on it, and you forget that it stresses you out when you're not working on it.

No, writing can be stressful in a it's-always-in-the-back-of-your-mind, stressing you out even when you're not actively thinking about it kind of way.

One of the first times this hit me was when I was fifteen years old, a sophomore in high school, and preparing for my first writing conference and professional critique. I was under a strict deadline to finish my pages and get them turned in—my first real deadline. I stressed every minute until I was in the car on the way home.

For me, there was so much riding on that conference. It was the first time I'd ever put myself out there as a writer. It was really the first time I'd said, "Writing is something I love. Something I want to do for the rest of my life."

And that was scary. There's something about claiming writing as a part of who you are that never stops being scary. Writing is subjective, and it leaves us vulnerable. When people reject our writing, it feels like they're rejecting pieces of *us*, because writing is an incredibly personal thing.

Almost two years after that first conference, I had another perspective-shifting moment. I was stressed about another "deadline"—this time I was waiting to hear back from an agent who had requested my full manuscript—and I caught myself wallowing about how hard it is to be a teen writer. Everyone was telling me, "You're not old enough. Just enjoy writing. Don't think about getting published just yet. You don't have the life experience." (And there is some merit to this, but it's not 100% correct.)

I knew that rejection was coming, and I was terrified of it. I was terrified of what would happen when I was told, this time by an industry professional, that I wasn't good enough.

But then, right in the middle of my wallowing, I had another thought. It was this moment of intense pride, like, "Wow. I wrote a book. A whole book." And I realized that I'd tried to do some new things—with characters, plot elements, my narrative—and it was hard. But I did it.

I'd written a book.

And I was truly, deeply in love with it.

And that was the moment that I knew that I'd be okay with the rejection when it came—and it did. But it didn't destroy me like I'd thought it would.

So my advice is simply this: *fall in love with your own work.* Fall deeply and terribly and passionately and unashamedly in love with writing—more than that, fall in love with telling stories. Because when people tell you that you're too young, that you're not good enough, that you'll never be good enough, that's what will keep you going. Not the praise, the allure of a publishing contract or fame, but the joy of telling in a story in the most beautiful way you know how—honestly.

It's like when people say the key to confidence is to love yourself. The key to writing confidence is to be in love with what you're working on. Because when you love it, it will show. It will shine through your words so brightly that no one will be able to look away.

With love,

Emily Vedder

Dear Writer,

Write about *everything*. The good things. The bad things. The things that make you rage against the world, the things that make you feel like you're on top of it, the things that make you want to hide in your closet and cry.

Writing about your feelings is some of the greatest freedom you'll ever find, but it can also be one of the scariest things you'll ever do. Because suddenly, when you record your feelings, when you put your thoughts into words, words with rhythm and atmosphere and emotion, they're real. They're out there. The written word is more permanent than thoughts floating around your brain. Written words have power. Written words can make people feel things. Written words can make *you* feel things.

Dear writer, please don't ever be afraid of your power.

Even if no one ever sees your writing, even if you never share it with anyone else, your words are powerful. They hold power for you—they're like little bookmarks in your life story, places you've been filled to overflowing with joy and had to let it out, so you spilled it onto a page, and places where you had nothing left to give but somehow managed to crank out a few lines.

Your words are powerful.

You are powerful.

Don't be afraid of it, and don't forget it.

All the best,

Emily Vedder

for the love of a word

"You can make anything by writing." -C.S. Lewis

There have never been truer words. Writing, I believe, is the only limitless medium. Everything else—sculpting, painting, drawing, is all limited in its own ways. Only in writing can you truly 'make anything', as Lewis said. You can create new worlds, new people, new objects, new rules, new laws of nature…

At face value, that can seem pretty intimidating. If you can do *anything,* then how are you supposed to do anything at all?

That probably sounds pretty silly, but let me put it in easier to understand terms. If you were faced with picking one ice cream flavor out of a zillion, how could you possibly even *begin* the process of choosing? Of narrowing it down? It would be so overwhelming. You'd probably end up picking the same flavor you've liked since you were five, or maybe the one that everyone has been raving about.

Now, take that example back into writing. The thought of picking one idea out of an infinite number of potential ones seems daunting to say the least. Your first instinct may be to write a story similar to those you've always read, or maybe write something in a genre that is flying off the shelves.

When I first began writing seriously, I was around ten. I started a novel called *Back To The Past.* It was about a young tween who somehow got sent back into the 1900s (I was highly inspired by a book I had recently read called *Anne Frank and Me* by Cherie Bennett and Jeff

Gottesfeld.). After hitting writers block about 20 pages in, I thought, well, everyone seems to like vampires now! Let me try that. Now I must say, I don't know why I thought that was a good idea when I didn't enjoy reading vampire books in the first place!

As you may have guessed, none of those books ever made it to even a first draft. I honestly believe that the reason they failed is because I was writing *somebody else's story*. Those stories I tried writing just weren't me. The key to writing, I've found, is to write what you love. Write something you'd read, something that speaks to you.

Recently, I managed to self-publish a novelette. It was my senior project. That story was the hardest I have worked on a piece of writing in my 18 years of life. It only totaled to 72 pages, but the story came from my heart and simply bloomed on paper. The characters feel so real, like flesh and blood. Like they're out there, I just haven't met them yet. Sometimes my protagonist slips to the forefront of my mind and I simply smile.

Once my characters took control, the book seemed to write itself. The story was always there; I just had to give my characters a means to get it out. This idea of stories seeming simply to *be* until an artist is brave enough to give them life reminds me of an amazing quote from Michelangelo: "I saw the angel in the marble and carved until I set him free."

If you are brave enough to find your story, do so unapologetically. Tell those stories that are clawing at your insides, begging to be released. Write in a flavor that no-one has ever tasted before; let your story taste of pain and

74

happiness and the sunshine after the storm. Make your reader throw your book down with a flourish and say, wow, that was so much *better* than chocolate.

Annie Kate Harley

for the love of a word

Dear Writer,

Don't wait for the inspiration to come. Don't sit and stare at the blank screen that beckons you into oblivion. Don't give in to the siren call of social media.

Write.

The words will be terrible. They will stammer and stutter and trip over themselves. They will thrash and scream and wail like background noises in a horror movie.

Add another sentence. Another paragraph. Watch as the words begin, one by one, to decode themselves and decide what they are and what they mean.

Write one more word.

Begin the story with "I have no idea what this story is supposed to end up looking like", and take a leap of faith. Trust that the story has a purpose and a reason for existing.

All the preparation in the world is no replacement for typing out "Once upon a time," and following it up with another word.

Love,

An Exasperated Writer

Annie Louise Twitchell

for the love of a word

A note to myself—

When the path seems too hard, when the journey seems too perilous, when the night seems too dark—

Remember that you have a paintbrush and that blackest night is only a blank canvas waiting to be littered with stars.

Remember that you have a pen and you can write a bridge to cross the chasm that threatens to engulf you.

Remember that you have an eraser and you can smudge out the sharp edges.

Remember that you are more than the work, and that the work is an outpouring of you.

There is a strange beauty in this lonely work. To create is to realize my connection with things greater than myself, and soon enough the work is not lonely at all, but blessed and beloved.

Remember this when the journey seems hard.

Annie Louise Twitchell

for the love of a word

To the child who was hurt:

Little one, I see how your hands tremble when you try to write your story. I know how the words burn like bile sometimes, and I know how the demons in the dark places try to subdue you.

Little one, I know that the pouring out of words gives sweet release. Pour them out into the secret places. Write them in a journal and fill the pages with the ugly, sickening things. Then burn it to ashes and nothingness. Grab hold of the rage before it sours into bitterness. There is a strange loneliness in the way the stars flicker and the words leak out from behind your eyelids.

Do not be afraid to capture the people who hurt you, and in your pages, burn them. Use the fear and the rage as the ink with which you write.

Do not allow them victory. They wish to break you, to silence you. You need never share the story with anyone else but do not let them silence you from yourself.

Let go. Do not let your heart turn cold. Let it burn with all the rage that the Son of God laid out. Let it rage against wrong, and when the fire is burned low, let it rest.

You are more than the things that have shaped you.

—from a writer who has wept

Annie Louise Twitchell

78

for the love of a word

Dearest,

It's a cold morning and I've just finished up some work. It seems like unimportant work sometimes in comparison to the work I want to do beside you, but I know it's important. The words are sometimes as far as away as you.

There are so many things I want to say to you. The words aren't here, in my fingers, as they usually are. Instead they fill my veins and make my heart race. I miss you with every fiber of my being, and I miss the places we've never been.

In my dreams and the secret places in my heart, I know what we will do. Helping people is written in our DNA. In some way, you and I will make a difference— whether it is one big difference or thousands of tiny differences, I don't know, but I know the world will not be the same after you and I are through.

My hands ache to be held. The cold seeps into my bones and makes my blood sluggish. Alone is my least favorite place to be.

I'm watching for you, always.

I hope the time is soon. I need you. Even the words are beginning to fail as company and comfort. I need you.

—from a writer in love

Annie Louise Twitchell

for the love of a word

Dear Writer,

Oh, love. I see you there behind the keyboard, hands to the ready, fingers itching to type, mind whirling with the story—or stories—you want to tell.

Three years ago I was just the same, dear writer. And today I am the same. The distance between today and three years ago is too great to tell.

Dear writer, I need you to know that this will possibly be the hardest thing you will do, and this is coming from a girl who has done, willingly, and more often unwillingly, many very hard things.

Love, this world is not kind. This world today does not see art the way we dreamers do. It is learning to, I believe, but only because it is lit with the passions of men who believed they could fly. The starry sky over my head tonight is flecked with traces of dreams that came true.

Dreamer, this world does not see with your eyes. It does not see the love, hope, passion, freedom, and grace that light up the room when you write. It does not see the pain, blood, tears, and sorrow poured out into the pages you cherish. It does not see how your heart bleeds ink, my love. It does not see the changing tides and the crescendo of the ocean in a path of moonlight.

This world is made of people like you and I, and sometimes... sometimes people are cruel. Sometimes people are angry. Sometimes people don't understand.

for the love of a word

I do not wish for you to expect cruelty, dear one, only to be aware that it is there. And that not only is it laid out with heavy hands and unseeing hearts, but sometimes it is laid out with sugar smiles and candy tricks.

Dreamer, too often our hearts are tender. I think it makes our task on this earth easier. We bleed stories, after all. I would not see you grow cold in your heart and mind. I would not see those hands grow still. I would not see those dreams die.

My love, this world is not kind. How can it be? It has known so much hurt, so much bitterness and strife. It too bleeds, but it doesn't know how to use its stories to heal.

Dearest writer, that is what I would wish for you. I wish that the stories you write, the stories you dream of, would be a part of something that heals. And love, it's okay if the thing that heals is yourself. You are a part of this world too, after all, and you too are worthy of healing and hope.

I do not mean for you to only write soft things, tender things, easy things. Setting a bone is not soft or easy, but it must be done for healing to happen well. Healing is not only soft cotton bandages and pastel flowers. Healing is gritted teeth and sharp edges and a scream that cuts through the air like a knife.

Dearest writer, this is what I wish for you.

for the love of a word

Write.

Allow yourself to be afraid, because oh my love, you will be so very, very afraid.

But do not let the fear destroy your dreams.

Do not let the cruelty of others break you. Grieve for it, always, but do not let it dictate your choices.

Be angry. Be hard. Be soft. Be loving.

Writer, be passionate, and in your passion, you can touch this world.

And with a touch, healing begins.

Annie Louise Twitchell

for the love of a word

for the love of a word

ABOUT THE
AUTHORS

CS Taylor was raised on the fairy lit roads somewhere between the backstreet alleys of Jackson, Mississippi, and the jazz infested avenues of New Orleans. Now she's settled in the open meadows of Iowa where the tulips grow thicker than the grass.

She spends her days teaching special needs and gifted children to read and write and spends her nights star gazing and ignoring her writing.

She graduated from Sterling College in 2016 with majors in Writing and Editing and Research Psychology. She graduated from University of Nebraska (Omaha) with her terminal degree in Writing and Editing in 2018.

thefoldedworld.wordpress.com
instagram.com/thefoldedworld
facebook.com/cherise.taylor.73307
pinterest.com/thefoldedworld
www.goodreads.com/user/show/81891766-cs-taylor.
thefoldedworld@gmail.com

for the love of a word

Emily Vedder has loved writing since she learned to type
with two fingers. As she moved on to typing with all ten,
her love for telling stories and crafting characters
continued to grow. She completed her first novel before
she finished high school, a YA contemporary mystery.
Emily is now working towards her degree in music therapy
at a university in Missouri. When she's not studying or
writing, she's probably reorganizing her bookshelf or
searching for weird socks at Target.

Lauren Grinder is the office manager and media director at Child Evangelism Fellowship (CEF) of Montana. She graduated from Montana Code School in 2017 and did her computer programming internship with Trans World Radio (TWR) in South Africa. She enjoys writing stories that push her imagination and show the growth that God has caused in her own life. Now Lauren enjoys teaching kids to program and does much of the office work at CEF of Montana along with running the website and promotional videos.

Lauren is always thrilled at the idea of God using her to share His love with others while using her unique talents.

C. F. Barrows is a former homeschooler who writes to grapple with tough issues and share the good news of Jesus Christ with her generation. She lives in Northern Indiana with her family and a freakishly well-behaved dog.

digressionsofademendescribe.blogspot.com

Rebecca Woodie is a student in fashion design who both designs and writes from her love of fantasy and adventure. Some of her other loves (which will hopefully get written into her stories someday!) are plants, snakes, crochet, reading, and long wandering walks through the woods.

instagram.com/rebecca.woodie.author

Rachel Katherine is a High School Graduate with a variety of interests, especially in creative pursuits such as upcycling, playing the ukulele, sewing, dancing, jewelry making, language learning and of course, writing.

rachelkatherine33@gmail.com

Kathy Twitchell lives in Western Maine with a heap of children, cats, and books. When asked to compose a biography, she came up with a second letter almost as long as the one she wrote for the book.

"This is so much harder than I thought it would be. It was easier to write a piece to be published than to compose a brief bio about myself, the author. I'm tempted to copy Anne McCaffrey, who once said she had green eyes, silver hair, and the rest was 'subject to change without notice.'

"Who Am I?
I am a daughter, I am a mother, I am a sister, I am a wife, I am a friend.
I am a writer, I am a reader, I am a learner, I am a teacher, I am a voice.
I am a child of the most high God, thoroughly enjoying my sojourn on earth.
I cannot keep my mouth shut. Even when I try, the words burst out with even more force, for the pressure of trying to keep them in. Sometimes I can see so clearly, these bubbles of inspiration that appear out of nowhere, random portions of truth. I love to write, to speak, to converse; I love to listen, to make connections, and to find beauty in the most unlikely of places."

literarylanternbearers.com

Melissa Holliday lives in the heart of Georgia, where she divides her weekdays between writing, blogging, sewing and crocheting- when she isn't gardening, painting or doing laundry- and her weekends between church and family time. She's a lover of all things Regency, Victorian and Vintage, and enjoys nothing more than watching black-and-white movies, sewing historical dresses, and sneaking slices of cheesecake and doughnuts to her desk when she's supposed to be writing. Although she hasn't met her Mr. Right yet, Melissa loves writing Christian romance novels while dreaming of her own 'happily ever after' one day and encouraging other young people to be patient in finding theirs, and though she isn't quite old enough yet to be considered a wise old maid, she loves giving advice on her blog from a big sister point of view, something which she knows quite a bit about doing as she is the oldest of seven children. If asked what her greatest accomplishment is, she'd say not being eaten alive by mosquitoes.

livingasaproverbs3130lady.blogspot.com/
facebook.com/livingasaproverbs3130lady/

for the love of a word

instagram.com/livingasaproverbs3130lady/

Keturah Lamb is a realistic idealist learning how to both live in and embrace God's reality and believes she can rationalize emotions with philosophy and politics. She has many passions in life; humanity and humor at the top of her list. She grew up in Missouri and currently lives in Montana but travels several times a year to visit friends who live too far away. Though her first love is writing, she cleans houses as she strongly believes artists shouldn't starve. She has three fairytales published in two anthologies: *Mythic Orbits Volume 2* and *The Fairytale* Riot. One of her novellas is a semi-finalist in ACFW's Genesis contest. You can read more of her work at keturahskorner.blogspot.com where she posts every Wednesday.

Twitter: @KeturahAbigail

for the love of a word

instagram.com/keturahlamb/
wattpad.com/user/KeturahLamb

Abigail M. Swanson is a writer and editor from San Diego, California. As an avid reader of all manner of books from a young age, her love of literature and story is deeply rooted in her earliest memories (she fondly remembers Jane Eyre as the first book that made her cry). She writes poetry and the occasional short fiction while she makes slow but steady progress on her novel, a retelling of ice-themed fairy tales and Russian folklore. When she's not lingering between the pages of a book (or e-reader), she enjoys sewing, fiddling, drawing, and drinking coffee. You can read about her eclectic adventures on her website.

AbigailMSwanson.com

Selina is a biologist-by-day, writer-by-night native of Pennsylvania. She lives with her husband, dog, and two cats and spends her time writing, reading, creating art, and dreaming about fictional worlds. She loves to write strong women and fantasy worlds, and she believes that stories connect us all. Besides writing and sciencing, Selina also runs an author support business, Paper Cranes, LLC, that provides editing, consulting, and mapmaking services to authors, writers, and students.

sjeckert.wordpress.com
Facebook: @selinajeckert
Twitter: @selinajeckert
Tumblr: @papercraneswriting

Annie Harley is a 18-year-old self-published author. Her hobbies include reading, writing, and drawing. In her free time, she loves playing cards with her boyfriend and sister, drinking Dunkin' Donuts, and praising Jesus. Harley is a devoted Christian. She plans on pursuing a degree in Communications with a focus in internet & social media from Regent University. Upon graduation from college, she hopes to become a youth pastor and social media strategist.

annieharley.com/
facebook.com/anniekateharley/
goodreads.com/author/show/18679146.Annie_Harley

Isabella Morganthal is a twenty-something author, dreamer, and child of God. She works in children & youth ministry, and is also a writing coach with Cheerleader Sessions. Isabella has been writing for almost fifteen years and loves to connect with other writers.

isabellamorganthal.weebly.com
facebook.com/isabellamorganthal
Instagram.com/isabellamorganthal

Savannah Jezowski lives in Amish country with her Knight in Shining Armor and a wee warrior princess. She is the founder of Dragonpen Designs and Dragonpen Press, which offer author services such as cover design, developmental edits, and interior formatting. Her debut novella "Wither" is featured in *Five Enchanted Roses,* an anthology of Beauty and the Beast, and is a prequel to *The Neverway Chronicles,* a Christian fantasy series filled with tragic heroes and the living dead. She is also the author of *When Ravens Fall,* a Norse Beauty and the Beast retelling, *The Witching Hour Series,* and *The Innkeeper's Wife.* She is featured in several Fellowship of Fantasy anthologies. When she isn't writing, Savannah likes to read books, watch BBC miniseries, and play with cover design. She also enjoys having tea with her imaginary friends.

dragonpenpress.com/
facebook.com/savannahjezowskiauthor/
instagram.com/savannahjezowskiauthor/

twitter.com/SavannahJez

Katherine Brown is a lover of books and weaver of words. Her first official publication was of two children's books in 2017, which has now grown into five books of the *School is Scary series*, soon to be finished with book six; however, she likes to think her career as a writer started when she sold her parents newsletters of articles about school and poetry for fifty cents per copy as a pre-teen.

Married to a wonderful husband and the mom of a smart, spunky stepdaughter, Katherine enjoys spending time with family and reading as many new books as she can get her hands on. Her YA series, the Ooey Gooey Bakery Mystery series, is ramping up in 2019 with book 1 *Rest, Relax, Run for Your Life* out in March and a brand-new release of book 2 *Pastries, Pies, & Poison* in June.

facebook.com/Katherine-Brown-Katie-Author-1007999836006370/

katherinebrownbooks.com
instagram.com/katherinebrownkatie/
amazon.com/Katherine-Brown/e/B078J72H8M

Annie Louise Twitchell is a homeschool graduate who is obsessed with dragons and fairy tales. She enjoys reading, writing, poetry, and many forms of art. When she's not writing, she can often be found reading out loud to her cat, rabbit, fish, and houseplants, or wandering barefoot in the area around her Western Maine home.

AnnieLouiseTwitchell.com
Annie-Louise-Twitchell.blogspot.com
Facebook.com/AnnieLouiseTwitchell
Instagram: @the_bookish_cat_dragon
Twitter: WriterAnnieLou

for the love of a word

for the love of a word

A Final Note:

The setting: a snowstorm in Western Maine, circa January 2019.

I had the rather crazy idea of writing a book of love letters for writers. After about 30 minutes of thought, I made a sign-up form for other people to add their submissions to my book. I had no idea what the plan was, just that this was something that needed to be done, and I could do it.

Talk about fear. This—For the Love of a Word—is everything I've been wanting for the last four years and a lifetime before that. And I felt too small and inadequate and undeserving.

To cut a long story short, fifteen people sent me some amazing pieces of writing, so I had to work through the fear. I'd promised them a book, and I had to get my act together and pull the pieces together. I adore each and every one of these authors, and I'm so excited to share the final collection with you.

To my writers: It's been a wild ride, but it wouldn't have been the same without you. Thanks for joining me on this journey.

With love,

Annie Louise Twitchell

52102943R00068

Made in the USA
Middletown, DE
08 July 2019